The Primı

and other poems

by
Bob Taylor

Illustrations by Gladys Hobson

The Primrose Path

And other poems

By

Bob Taylor

Copyright © Arthur Robert Taylor

ISBN 0-9548885-4-5

First Published April 2007

Magpies Nest Publishing

Further copies may be ordered from:

Magpies Nest Publishing

primrose@magpiesnestpublishing.co.uk

www.magpiesnestpublishing.co.uk

Contents:

This book is dedicated to my darling wife Linda.

In gratitude for all her patience and support, for putting up

with my idiosyncrasies, my bad temper, my chauvinism,

my sexism,

my laziness in matters of domestic chores, my tendency to

give her dyspepsia; and to whom I

give my undying love and devotion.

Bob

My thanks to Sheila who taught me 'no pain — no gain'.

Also to Gladys Hobson for beating me into submission in

order to produce this book

and

for the cover and illustrations.

And to Simon Hobson for preparing the book for printing.

Lament of the Old Soldier

My Muse has nowhere left to go,
Except the place where soft winds blow.
I don't remember winters there,
Perhaps she's taking greater care
And, thinking of my ancient bones,
She only seeks for lighter tones,
(Not the sirens — how *they* sounded!)
Yes, life back there seemed far more rounded.
Marriage vows bound us together
Until the day we died — forever!
.

We went to war with good intent,
Not realizing what it meant.
A winter here? Oh, no — that's swallowed
By the other things that followed;
The comradeship of men in plight
Ensures such memories have no bite.
We still have meetings, though we're now few,
And none of us prefer the new.
We reminisce on things we've done —
Tell tales of how we beat the Hun.

A haunting tune, 'Lily Marlene',
I whistled, softly, down country lane
When I returned to civvy life,
And took a stroll there with my wife.
My two boys, who were on her knee
When I went far across the sea,
Had quite grown up, and the youngest lad
Had no idea I was his dad.
Welcome home? 'Well, don't you dare
To sit in granddad's favourite chair!'

Ration books were still around,
Though things went further then, we found;
No need for shopping trolleys full.
And, yes, I know that this sounds dull,
But neighbours would pass teapots over
The garden wall to help each other;
And everyone on my whole street
Smiled at each other when they'd meet.
(My Muse, discordant things has found,
And colder winds begin to sound).

Did this younger generation,
Who vented lust to satiation,
Ever find a worthwhile goal?
They lived for Sex and Rock & Roll,
And pleased themselves, whether right or wrong,
Without paying The Piper for his song;
Left shattered families strewn around,
And few of them seem to have found
That there's a payment in the end.
The Piper always wins, my friend.

Bus Stop Conversation '64

I'm sorry, friend, but I am not
The kind of girl you think you've got,
For daddy's told me of *your* kind,
And I prefer a *loving* mind.

What's that I hear — you want to marry?
Oh, I'm afraid you'll have to tarry
Until we're well and truly wed —
You'll get it on our marriage bed!

And yes, I *am* a virgin still —
It's all a matter of the will.
Snigger all you like, and mock it,
But I don't *care* what's in your pocket!

A single peck upon my cheek
Is all you get from me this week —
For other things, you'll have to roam.
Goodnight, my friend — I'm going home!

Musical Degeneration

I love melody and harmony,
But discordance and cacophony,
Is all one seems to hear these modern days.
When the mind needs an ablution,
Music is a fine solution —
Especially when it's heard on 'Songs of Praise'.

But my daughters think so different:
'Music must be all-insistent!'
And they never seem to care of consequences.
This one thought gives me the shudders:
Perhaps one day they'll both be mothers!
By then I hope I've lost all auditory senses.

But there may be consolations,
And I pass this information
To sufferers, with whom I am in kind:
If the awful din their kids make
Gives them both a constant headache,
Then I, for one, will probably not mind!

Little Miss Prissy '64

Ronnie's left the pub again
To walk that girl home; what's the game?
'Her dad's asked me to be her friend
And see her home through Donkey Lane.'

We'd both seen her quite early on
Before she went to Carcroft dance.
Upon her face dismay was written:
'Please, this is my only chance.'

'OK', said Ronnie, 'I'll be there;
I'll wait for you and walk you home,
But until then, just you take care.'
Is his brain of solid bone?

She seems to me a prissy miss,
The kind who says: 'Oh, please don't touch!'
He won't even get a kiss.
I think she's asking far too much.

So here I am, left all alone,
The landlord's putting on the towel;
Now, who's that girl there on her own?
I think I'll take a little prowl.

I suppose that she's now tucked in bed,
While I'm laid here amid the dew
With all my passions drained and dead,
And wishing I was in mine, too.

Catch a Falling Karaoke Star

I *would* have put her in my pocket,
But I had no means to lock it;
For stardust is a precious thing —
What others need to help them sing!

So we put her in a wheelie-bin;
She lit up all the space within!
But then the evidence we hid,
By simply closing up the lid.

When the taxi finally came,
She didn't even know her name.
We gently locked her in the boot —
She didn't seem to give a hoot!

She said she woke up, in the morning,
Full of anguish, full of yawning;
But, in the sky, when evening came,
I saw her twinkling again.

Childhood Innocence?

This baby suckling from his mother
Will build a rigid Iron Curtain.
He'll try to say that he's my brother,
But I'll deny it — that's for certain.
He'll say: 'A million deaths is *a* statistic!'
What makes a baby turn sadistic?
Joseph Stalin —
He's a darlin'!

This young boy playing by the river
With blue eyes shining, open wide,
Will one day cause the world to shiver;
He'll start a war, bring genocide
To millions in a Holocaust;
But, now, he's innocent — of course.
Little Adolph —
Take your hat off!

This young girl singing at the door,
With pretty ribbons in her hair,
Will bury children on the moor,
And chill all mothers with her stare.
What happened to her Christmas mirth?
You'll find it in the Yorkshire earth.
Myra Hindley —
Oh, so spindley!

And me? I don't think I'm so bad,
But I was no innocent — I know;
I remember all the thoughts I had
Which I was careful not to show;
And perhaps I would have indulged *my* senses
If it had not been for consequences.

Floral Smiles

A smile can be a pretty rose
That decorates the face,
And when it blossoms slowly,
It gives it added grace.

Sometimes it's like a daffodil,
Bright and cheerful — jolly;
At other times it's sultry,
Like a Lily-of-the valley.

A smile is many flowers,
Depending on the seeds,
But there are some that harbour malice
And these are of the weeds.

Beware of Deadly Night-shade
And its floral decoration;
There is no humour in this smile,
Just cunning machination.

Journey to the Land of Milk and Honey

I was happy here, and wished to stay,
But something's driving me away;
My little home is getting smaller —
Or is it me that's growing taller?

The silken voice I loved to hear
Is screaming at me now, I fear;
The gentle, rhythmic, thumping sound
Has lost its reassuring pound.

It's started beating far too quick,
And making me feel rather sick.
All around I feel compression —
It sure is giving me depression.

I'm trying now with all my might
To reach that tiny chink of light;
I've never noticed it before —
Perhaps it is a little door!

I've got my head through — that's OK,
Now I can see the light of day,
But something's tickling my chin —
I think I'd better go back in!

Oh-oh, I find I can't reverse —
I should have put my arms through first;
And now it seems that I'm stuck tight.
I'm really in a dreadful plight.

Someone's pulling on my head.
Oh! How I wish that I were dead;
They're smacking me upon my bum —
Have I been doing something wrong?

I'm happy now — it's rather pleasant.
You'd think I was some kind of present.
I sleep all day till lights go out,
Then for my loving mum I shout.

Don't need to do a lick of work —
I must confess I have to smirk;
I'm in a Land of Milk and Honey —
It's nicer here than in her tummy.

Not Alone

Don't ever think you are alone,
Wherever you may be,
For you will find my spirit there
To keep you company.

And he will whisper in your ear
The sweetest words he knows,
Whenever you're depressed,
Or whenever you repose.

When rough and cold winds blow,
You will feel his warm embrace,
And his kisses will bring colour
To your sad and pretty face.

And all the memories you have
Of me when I was kind,
He'll open up the door to them,
To soothe your troubled mind.

A Smile

A smile is so much more than
Gentle curving of the mouth,
The edges moving North,
And the middle moving South;
It is the eyes that have it,
With a twinkle or a stare:
With the former you relax,
And with the latter you beware.

Through the eyes you see the spirit,
Whether joyful, mean or sad,
And the mouth is just a tool we use
For either good or bad.
Malicious minds can hang a smile
Upon their pretty face,
But the Windows of the Soul display
Their utter lack of grace.

Avarice and envy
Can be seen within them too:
Lurid greed shines brashly,
And resentful eyes are cool.
Sly cunning has a telling mark:
Eyes dart from side to side;
If you watch for all these signs you'll find
Mean spirits cannot hide.

But then there is another creed,
A different point of view:
A smile can be that mask you need
To hide the real you;
A soul that cries in sorrow
For a world that is insane;
For the poor there's no tomorrow —
Only work and grief and pain.

A smile will hide a breaking heart
To protect those held most dear
From the knowledge of their sadness,
And the gripping hand of fear.
A smile is like a running stream
That splashes on its way:
Refreshing drops of water
On the desert of the day.

But for now let's think of simple things
And dwell upon the pleasure,
For the joy an honest smile can bring
Is surely without measure.
Love, warmth, hope, and kindness —
Harmless humour's in there too —
All of them, in their own way,
Paint on their special hue.

The Primrose Path

Just Good Friends

There is a lady I know well
Whom I could kiss — she would not tell;
But she is married to another,
And I am not her darling brother.

If it were so, my heart would beat
A different drum when ere we meet,
Nor would it harbour melodies, so tender;
These are things that she engenders.

The irony is — I'm wedded too
And I'll remain forever true.
For nothing here is underhand,
No loving that we both had planned.

For spirits touch when ere they meet —
They find a different way to greet;
And softer kisses give each other.
I would not wish to be her brother.

Female spirits cannot thrive,
And they do not feel alive
Unless they've someone to be there for —
A rougher spirit they can care for.

For perfect skin is more a splendour
If there's a minor flaw to render
Comparison against each another.
I suppose the truth is that I love her.

The word that I have mentioned here,
Has many meanings, some unclear:
Yes, love can mean so many things —
But mine is like fresh hillside springs.

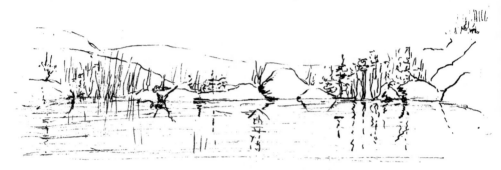

Within the Pauses

What does she think of within the pauses,
When her head turns away and her eye-lashes dip
As she studies her nails? What causes
The gleam in her eyes as she nibbles her lip?
Then she looks around with a toss of her head
And breathes a sigh so long and drawn out.
Is it what somebody's done or what somebody's said
That's turned her pretty mouth into a pout?

Now she looks at her glass with its contents so clear
And she takes a sip with eyes looking around
At the rest of the crowd who are sitting quite near;
And she smiles to herself at something she's found.
She leans for her cigarette pack and her lighter,
And she smokes with her fingernails shining so vain.
Her friend gives her a nudge and she starts looking brighter;
Now she's laughing and joking all over again!

She

She's very shy and insecure
And takes politeness to extremes;
But of one thing I'm very sure —
She's never what she seems.

She's pretty and she knows it too,
And though she's never been a flirt,
She doesn't mind a glance or two —
Providing they're not pert!

She cares for people who are down
And doesn't mind a bit of dirt;
I've never seen her wear a frown —
Always tries hard not to hurt.

She spends a lot of time in thought
While washing pots or ironing clothes;
I've never seen her overwrought —
She's gracious, I suppose.

I think God's given her to me,
If only for a little while,
To let me know how I should be —
And show me how to smile!

Spirits Need No Decoration

Her eyes, so bright, can look so dull
And glazed when her weak body fails.
It's then I feel my heartstrings pull —
And sweet compassion all-prevails.

I find her at her prettiest
When her hair is lank and without care.
In jeans and jumpers she looks best —
There is a meaning here, somewhere.

For ornament and painted face,
And pretty clothes, cannot enhance
Her earthy beauty in my gaze.
She's always worth a second glance.

I know what happens deep inside
Her mind, where I have often been,
And I love the thoughts that there reside.
Her spirit shines, is what I mean.

The body will crumble and wrinkle soon,
Clothes and ornaments will fade,
But lovely spirits stay at noon,
Forever dressed in white brocade.

Her Voice

Her voice — how soft and warm the tones
That thrill me to my very bones.
Her words — though clipped — are sweet to me
And never will they cease to be.

I find her plain and Yorkshire grammar
Gives her a kind of added glamour;
And she is such a pretty lass…
I think the answer's in my past.

My thoughts of Maggie and the mill
(Though I was young they linger still),
Of how she drowned in the river Floss,
Gave me a sense of grief and loss.

But now she's come to me again,
And her spirit hovers, until when
I know not; but this I know —
I will not ever let her go!

Green-eyed Lady

When her eyes twinkle, I can see
What's happening inside her mind;
I know that, now, she's filled with glee;
She also is so very kind.

But, when they soften and fill with dew,
I fancy I can see her soul.
It's then I know she loves me, too —
Though friendship is her only goal.

I think she knows that my heart aches —
And friendship thrives at times like this,
But to see such sadness often makes
Me want to seal it with a kiss.

Coffee Break

Through crowded streets we walk alone,
With busy shoppers everywhere,
And none of them must ever know
The thoughts I have, and what we share.

I want to hold her in my arms
And kiss her softly, touch her face;
Enjoy the music of her charms
Which sing to me of tranquil grace.

Instead, I stop and turn, and say,
'Let's go for coffee — anywhere.
I've had enough of this today —
Let's try that café over there.'

Across the table I can see
The one I simply want to hug.
Her big eyes look across at me
Through steamy mists from coffee mug.

I listen to her endless chatter,
And watch her animated style,
But the only thing that really matters
Is that she is mine for just a while.

Such simple pleasures, I have found
Give to my life a pleasant glow.
Our spirits are together bound
Wherever we may go.

Windscreen

What makes my windscreen beautiful?
When last I looked it just seemed dull.
The landscape seemed to wear a frown,
As I watched the setting sun go down.

It's nearly gone behind the earth,
But now the skies glow and give birth
To dappled clouds with golden lining.
I muse on this as I'm reclining.

The pigmentation was all there
Before, yet when I looked it just seemed bare;
But then I caught her loving smile,
And now I find myself beguiled.

The twilight's here, and in its glow,
I nestle close to her; I know
Tranquillity within my soul
As church-bells swing and gently toll.

Twilight Lady

The golden globe is going down;
It hovers over the forests to the west
As if it's putting on its gown
Before it settles down to rest.

And as it sinks below the trees,
The glow, which on the clouds it casts,
Brings shadows of eternity,
And memories from my past.

How many times have I been here,
With different ladies by my side
To watch the same star disappear,
And bring on eventide?

But all thoughts of others my mind spurns —
I've found true love this time;
And only she has ever turned
My thoughts into a rhyme.

Land of Never-Never

When first I saw her cheerful smile
I thought, 'She's such a pretty lass.'
Before I'd even walked a mile
All thoughts of her were in the past.

The months rolled by and every time
We met she seemed to smile for me;
My thoughts turned into silly rhyme —
As if she'd turned a rusty key.

What's happened since, I'm not quite sure;
Why do I feel this way?
I cannot seem to find a cure —
Perhaps I never may.

The glow I feel when she is near
Fulfils my very soul;
And absences fill me with fear —
My mind won't let her go.

And every time we meet together
I know that I must leave
This wondrous Land of Never-Never,
As inwardly I grieve.

Where Friendship Ends

So soft and warm is her embrace,
And different from her cheerful smile
Which lights up all her pretty face;
For now there is a kind of guile
Mixed in with all her tenderness;
And sadness, for I see the furrows
Upon her brow. She seeks an end to loneliness
Without the guilt that surely follows.

I know her well — or so it seems;
I see through glimpses all she's thinking,
From worried frown to joyful beams;
But now I fear she's only sinking.
And I am, too. I don't know where
I'm really going with my friend;
I only know I want to share
These moments with her — 'til they end.

Wedding
Bells
½ mile

Friendship
Ends
1 mile

In Cabal

Laughing, joking — merriment,
The clock strikes twelve, and still they sing;
But once their money's all been spent
Mine Host will give his bell a ring.

And, as they're strolling to their homes,
Couples, arm in arm to show
To others that they're not alone,
They keep their voices hushed … and low.

Deformed, and savage Caliban,
The squalid, dark and twisted beast
That lurks within the heart of Man,
Is gorging on his latest feast:

'Did you see that look she gave to him while they were
dancing?'

'I did, my dear, it's shocking what one sees when one is
glancing.'

'And the way his hand touched hers as they were briefly
interlocking?'

'I saw it all, my dear … do you think that they were
mocking?'

'That hard-faced hussy sits so quiet — she must have lots
of gall …'

'I've never heard her speak a word of anyone at all!'

'She even had the brazen nerve to drive him to his home!'

'And before he left the toilets, dear, I watched him use his comb …'

'It's disgusting how the likes of them ignore all our conventions …'

'Dancing with another's spouse, and drawing our attentions!'

'They'll come a cropper that's for sure — they'll never get away

With showing such contempt for all the good things that we say …'

Strands of Gold

Strands of gold that fall across my face,
And lips that hide a secret smile;
Her body moves with easy grace
As fingers probe me, to beguile.
Her dark eyes promise satisfaction
As moonbeams through her gold hair shine;
I know she watches my reaction
As I lie here, quietly supine.

Never Ending

Her breasts fall slowly into mine,
And settle there as I recline;
I feel her hair caress my cheek,
And listen to her softly speak;
I sense the beating of her heart —
Knowing its tenderness, in part;
And now my soul is filled with perfect peace
From which I never want release.

If only we could stay forever,
Without a movement or endeavour,
With passion slow and softly burning,
And never striving for, or turning
To, a storm where there's an ending;
Where passion dies and thoughts start wending
To worldly things that matter less
Than this, her warm and gentle press.

Waking Thoughts

Am I in love?
I only know, when I awake,
She is the first thing on my mind
And, though not fully conscious, make
A move towards her as I find
Her scent that lingers;
And I caress her with my fingers.
She is my dove.

Does she love me?
I open up my sleepy eyes,
And find that hers look into mine
With tenderness, and no surprise,
As if she's watched me all this time.
Sleep's separation is now gone,
I realize that she's the one;
And so does she.

The Rose Without a Thorn

A rose without a thorn
Would be so beautiful and grand,
But it would soon be ruined
By a rough and careless hand.

The thorns are for protection,
And if you feel the need
To hold it closer to you,
You must do it tenderly.

Some would use a velvet glove,
And others gloves of metals;
The purposes are just the same —
To crush its pretty petals.

My darling rose has thorns
But I don't need any glove —
I circumvent the need of them
By using Hands of Love.

And, during moments tender,
A new hybrid is born;
The ultimate perfection —
A rose without a thorn.

Familiarity

What's happened to the melody
That she once played upon my heartstrings?
Where has it gone — the symphony
That caused my soul to soar and sing?
The one I loved is still the same
But when I look at her I know
That something's gone; the kindled flame
Is flickering and burning low.

She still is kind — and thoughtful too,
And just as pretty as before;
But today I find that my mind's view
Has simply changed, and now I'm bored.
Why do I always find that love grows cold?
Perhaps I'd better stay, this time,
For after all — I'm getting old,
And friends are getting hard to find.

The Fire's Gone Out

The fire's gone out in my living room,
With white ash in the hearth, like frost;
I'm sitting alone within the gloom,
Thinking of all that I have lost.

It's twelve o'clock, the wife's in bed,
Sleeping on her gin and dry;
I think I'll stay down here instead
And have another drink of rye.

Then, hopefully, I'll fall to sleep
And dream of how it used to be
Before I made that fatal leap,
And Joan agreed to set me free.

Susan's younger in my dreams,
With pretty green eyes shining bright,
Smiling lips, and hair that seems
To shimmer in the morning light.

Oh, how I love the way she sings …
Or, maybe, Joan will visit me!
Long, black hair, like raven's wings,
And blue eyes twinkling, filled with glee …

'I'm coming, dear!' It's getting cold,
And Susan will have warmed the quilt;
I need these comforts, now I'm old —
It helps to soothe away my guilt …

The Last Waltz

The dance is almost over,
And here I am again —
Entwined with yet another,
Until I know not when.

They all seemed to have a glamour,
Which promised something more,
But now their silent clamour,
Only chills me to the core.

I should have persevered
With the one I married first,
But my passion disappeared
And I had to slake my thirst.

All My Ladies had a trait
For springing new surprises
Which I never could anticipate,
Nor penetrate the guises.

I wouldn't mind oblivion,
Where all things are negated:
No grief for any loved one,
No thought of those I hated.

I would gladly spend eternity
Unaware of my condition:
No thoughts of my infirmity,
No regrets, and no perdition.

For the ones I've loved, I've also pained,
And to dwell upon this ache,
Forever to it chained,
Is a path I'm loath to take.

The music's stopped; the drum is stilled;
She whispers in my ear:
'Let this, our meeting, be fulfilled —
It's time to leave, my dear.'

Honey Moon

A grey-haired couple, hand in hand,
Stroll silently across the sand;
They gaze in wonder at the rising moon,
And listen to the ocean's tune.
He softly whispers, 'I love you.'
How do I know their love is new?

They've learnt the lessons of the past,
And know, this time, that love will last;
Childrearing's done, all cause of strife
Is absent now in this new life;
And mature years have compensations.
But what of previous relations?

With offspring they have contact still —
Can take or leave them at their will.
Their problems, maybe, help sort out —
If convenient, no doubt;
Mistakes they made are far behind …
But don't they linger in the mind?

Do I envy those two there,
Who express affection with such care?
The answer's here — and this is Truth —
I've been there many times in youth,
But I found love that lasts forever
Is forged through hardships and endeavour.

End

Mysterious Place

There is a place of mystery
That never sees the light of day;
The source of mankind's history —
And problems, some might say.

Yes, men would sacrifice their brother
For the pleasure it provides.
It is the goal for every lover,
Where his passion flares and dies.

Can mortal Adam truly know
The secrets that reside therein,
Without a willing guide to show
Him how to turn the lock within?

For the final tumbler only turns
If Eve has given him the key;
All its mysteries he then learns —
Midst sighs, and groans, and ecstasy …

Taylor the Rat

Taylor was a little rat
Who lived in Rosie's garden,
And when she asked him if he'd leave,
He said, 'I beg your pardon?'

Now … Rosie has a soft spot
For all rats who have good taste,
So she fed him with ripe corn,
And he gobbled it with haste.

Well … Taylor grew so fat
That he couldn't move at all,
So she brought him in the house,
And she asked the vet to call.

By the time the vet arrived next day,
Poor Taylor had grown thinner,
And a dozen *little* Taylors
Were now tucking into dinner …

Poems of Redemption

Weighing Scales

Weighing scales are measures,
And we're careful how they lean,
But there's Sin and there's Perfection,
And there's nothing in-between.

You can do the nicest things,
And be oh so very kind,
But can you stop what's happening
Inside you're troubled mind?

A single thought that hatches
One solitary plot,
That contravenes God's Holy Law,
Will jeopardise the lot.

Some people weigh the good they do,
And then they weigh the bad,
But listen to me, my dear friend:
There's no comfort to be had.

For any good thing that you do
Is only through God's Grace,
And you'll only have the bad to show,
When you meet Him face to face.

The cross that Jesus died on,
Was not a pair of scales,
It was fixed and it was rigid,
And was fastened with some nails.

All the dying thief need do
Was look across to Him,
And ask Him for forgiveness,
To take away his sin.

There is a helpful pattern,
Which you'll need to think upon —
It's written in God's Holy Word,
In Numbers twenty-one.

There are corresponding verses
In John's Gospel, Chapter three;
I know you'll find them useful —
They helped to convince me.

Faith is in the head —
But it's also in the heart,
And you need it in *both* places
In order to take part.

Night Nurse

Hustle–bustle in the night,
Stolen moments in the staff-room,
Telling jokes in subdued light;
Then interrupted by the groan
Of one who needs the lavatory —
Not always getting there in time.
Familiar with indignity
And soiled beds of those who'd known
Ecstasy when in their youth;
But now they sickly dribble
From wrinkled corners of their mouth.
Sunken chins are wet with spittle.

Yet walking home on frosty mornings,
To see stars spangling like diamonds,
Can send her spirit upward soaring —
Taken to another mooring
Of serenity and wonder.
She anchors there amid her ponder.
In warmer seasons, twilight breaking,
Birds that twitter, think of mating;
Flowers blossoming, their sweet perfume,
Still heavy with the morning dew,
Gives life a new and special meaning.
Her body straightens from its leaning.

Just think how marvellous it will be,
When all our spirits are set free
From the bondage of our bodies,
To see the Heaven where our God is,
Forever free from every chain
That binds us all to the mundane.
Unless it works the other way,
And, no doubt thoughtless, we might stray
Into a world where Soul is absent —
No respite from grief and torment;
Wrinkles and incontinence,
Our dull and grave inheritance.

Heavenly Trinity

Last night, as the moon passed by my window,
It cast its beams upon my bed,
And as I lay there in its glow,
An understanding filled my head;
For I could see the Trinity,
How God is One and yet is Three.
God does say: look upon my world
And mysteries will be unfurled.

The sun, unseen, is God the Father —
Awe inspiring, burning bright,
The moon, His Son who came to gather —
A reflection of His Father's light;
The Holy Spirit's represented
By the light beams that have entered
Through my eyes into my mind,
And sometimes in my heart, I find.

The sun is far away in space,
But its rays are blinding to the eyes;
The moon is nearer, yet its face
Is tranquil, though of equal size;
The Sun gives life through radiation —
God's Spirit works in every nation;
The Moon rules the tides and commands the seas.
It all makes perfect sense to me.

Where Did I Begin

Where did I begin, and how?
Was it in the morning,
On a cold February day,
Or was it late at night
After drinks at the local pub?
Or in an air-raid shelter?
Or in the back seat of a car?

What lustful thoughts accompanied my conception
As my father's wriggling sperm
Penetrated the fatness
Of my mother's egg?

What happened to their passion for each other?
Was I the cause?
Did he whisper 'I love you,'
Or did she have to settle
For the groans of passion spent?

How will I end, and where?
Will it be at dawn that I take my leave
From all that binds me
To this earth?
Or during the day,
While reading a book?
Or watching television?
Will my body be racked with pain,
And shall I welcome death
And its release
From all my agony?

Will it be when I'm old
And grey,
Or will fate take me surprise
As I'm driving
Along the highway?

Will the one I love be there?
Or shall I die alone
And unloved
By anyone?

Will I really care?
Or shall I grieve upon the matter?

Where will I go?
Will I go back
To being nothing — as before?
Or will it be the start
Of a new journey
That never ends?

Will she be by my side
As I walk
Through Eternity ?
Or shall I walk alone
Without anyone to comfort me
On my travels?

Shall I see my God?
I sometimes tremble at the thought …

Adam's Dinner

My wife has gone and burnt my dinner,
And that is why I'm getting thinner.
She does this often, and won't take the blame
For the wasting of my frame.

So I say, 'This is why I am so thin,'
And throw the lot into the bin!
She wants to know why I am late!
Why can't she anticipate?

If she was more flexible,
Then I WOULD NOT BE IRRITABLE!
When I come home I want it ready —
She could do it nice and steady.

And if it happens that I'm early,
There's nothing to it — cook it nearly.
Of course, I want it all just so,
And if it's not — I'll let her know!

Conclusion

I know that all you ladies there
Are shouting, 'Rubbish — it's not fair!
Isn't it just like a man,
To deny all blame and pass the can?'

There is a template, plain and true,
For all the things that we men do;
It's written down in God's own book,
Right at the start — just take a look:

'Why did you eat from yonder tree?'
> 'It was this woman *you* gave *me*!'

Changing Emotions

Emotions are a strange brew;
They're at their rawest when we're new.
Indulged children, are they thankful?
It seems to me they often rankle!

Feelings can be effervescent —
Especially in the phase pubescent.
And even the most squalid dreams
Can make us wake up quite serene.

But things do change as we move through time;
We hide them now, they're more refined —
Unless our objectives are thwarted;
Then we rant until *that is* sorted!

In old age we have several choices
To meditate on — all the voices.
Which emotions do we cherish?
If noble ones, we may not perish …

Judgement and Redemption

I remember this — and mark it well:
The God *I* know went down to hell,
To the lowest dungeons of that ancient fortress,
Until his body was raised from rigor mortis.
He preached among that dreadful host
Who have no hope of which to boast.
To show them what they could have been
If they had only looked, and seen
The errors of the way they'd lived
Before the substance of their life was sieved
By the one who'd suffered more than they
Would ever do, or dare to say.

His grief was such, I'll never know;
I will not reap what I did sow,
Because I looked upon His cross
And counted love for Him not loss;
His Goodness and His Purity
Will never fail to cover me;
And all my sins, and all my woe
Will all be covered up like snow.

Soul and Spirit

So you think you have a soul, my friend,
To be with you forever;
You have a spirit, *and* a soul,
But they may not stay together.

Perhaps they're both extinguished
When your mortal life is done,
And they're buried with you in the grave,
Or burnt in crematorium?

While you still have a breath, my friend,
They together intertwine;
The spirit's yours and yours alone,
But the soul's from the divine.

And when you die God takes it back,
When lacking redeeming grace —
Of Christ's atoning sacrifice
For men of every race.

Broken Spirit

Just one small face among the crowd
Of people going into chapel,
It seems to say: 'Am I allowed?
I've only eaten *just one* apple.'

'Perhaps I'm wrong and there were more,
I *do* lose track of things.
I never added up the score;
Do these things cause my sufferings?'

She sits there quietly in the pew
And listens to God's Holy Word.
'But what am I supposed to do?' —
Thinking of what she has just heard.

'Can I just sing a hymn or two,
And say some prayers I really mean?
I'm sure these things can't fail to please you;
I'll do some good deeds in-between.'

A small voice whispers in her ear:
'A broken and a contrite spirit
Is all I ask. You need not fear,
For I am here, and *I* will fill it.'

End

The Drunkard's Lament

It only took one glass of wine
To make me feel this way;
I simply cannot yet define
The reason for this sway.

Of course, I'd had a few before,
They made me feel quite good,
So I told the barman 'Just one more!'
Now I'm staggering like a dud.

Why can't I simply stop at
The one that makes me peak?
Why does the bubble have to pop?
The answer I must seek.

Response

The advice that I can give to you,
I hope you mark it well:
Moderation is a heavenly thing —
Self-indulgence leads to hell!

Reflection in a Mirror

Good morning, mirror on the wall …
Oh! I'm not looking good at all!
Rheumy eyes with bags beneath,
Shrunken lips and rotting teeth.
Are you telling me the truth?
What have you done with all my youth?
If I'd looked into you less,
Would I still be at my best?

Could you possibly be lying,
When you say my hair needs dyeing?
There's definitely *something* wrong
For in my mind the same old song
Still comes to me when she is near —
It's just as haunting, just as clear;
And my heart still beats as fast
As ever it did in the past.

When I look at her I see
The pretty girl who promised me
That she'd be mine for ever more
When first we kissed outside her door.
Perhaps it's all inside my mind,
For after all, love is so kind —
It smoothes out wrinkles in the skin,
And looks at loveliness within.

The Dregs of the Summer Wine

The last of the dregs of the Summer Wine
Are almost drunk — you're fifty-nine!
Another year and they'll all be gone;
You'll be in your dotage, my old son.

The years are passing, it's getting late,
The hair is grey upon your pate,
But do not fret, and do not moan,
Just think of this — you're not alone!

The boys and girls you knew when young,
The Sons and Daughters of the throng
Of students with you in the class,
Have also nearly drained the cask.

The years are rolling so much faster,
And soon we'll face The Great Web-Master.
Some will stand, and some will fall —
I'm hoping that *you* get The Call.

But if you don't, I have to say,
I enjoyed the times we got to play
Together for a little while;
You always helped to make me smile.

Crown of Splendour

She's a girl I knew from times long gone —
I saw her once, or twice back then;
Her hair *was* brown, but now it's blonde.
Peroxide's done its job again?

What's underneath? Perhaps it's grey?
It's such a profound mystery;
Perhaps it's silver — who can say?
I'll look into her history!

She looks so young but she has years,
For I can count them and I know;
And what about her many tears
That took away life's pleasant glow?

And hardships, too — they take a toll,
Although she now seems cheerful;
But worry withers follicles;
Of answers I am fearful.

I must resist temptation —
I must not further dig,
For I've just this minute realised
It might only be a wig!

Domestic Bliss

Washing, washing everywhere;
Cups and saucers in the bowl;
Dirty pots and pans that stare …
Oh — Arsenal's scored another goal!

All my jumpers are still damp,
Not a clean shirt anywhere;
Me? I'm looking like a tramp!
Does this woman *really* care?

Out of fresh food now it seems;
I'm so hungry I could die;
She's still living in her dreams:
'Go microwave another pie.'

All I get these days are grumbles …
Oh — Arsenal's won! I'm feeling better;
But it will pass — my stomach rumbles;
Sometimes I wish I'd never met her!

The Promise Poems

Sheila the Cruel

My Inbox sighs when she pops in,
And trepidation fills my heart
As I'm scanning through the preview pane.
She's tearing all my work apart,
And my patience now is wearing thin;
She *says* that I must start *again*!

A fellow student, in my youth,
Her major skills were games and sport;
But now she's skilled at being cruel!
I only asked her for support,
And to show me how to *tell the Truth;*
But all she says is: I'm a fool!

Tenses wrong, and misplaced 'Buts';
Split infinitives, and adverbs
Which do not exist in her thesaurus;
Her criticism only serves
To depress me as she cuts
Me with the censure in her chorus.

But — if I persist in my endeavours
And don't allow her to seduce me
With her *correct* female style,
She'll need to put away her leathers,
When I receive my First Book fee;
Then it will be *my* turn to smile!

Yippee!

The Pigs That Fly!

Oh, little planet, third from the Sun,
So sterile and barren, but your time will come;
Within four billion years, you'll give birth to a mind
That will build rocket ships, and leave you behind.

A mind that has knowledge of Good and Evil,
Which will one day look back at your condition primeval;
It will gaze in wonder at your beauty profound,
And upon theories abundantly it will expound.

Soon you will cool, and oceans will form
To cover your mantle; then begins the New Dawn!
There's no need for a God to work a Great Plan —
It all starts with a 'mite', and not with a man.

A creature, so tiny, formless, and flaccid,
Constructed of 'strings' of amino acids;
DNA molecules contained in a spiral …
Does anyone know how *they* make an arrival?

Random events, and the sun's radiation,
Will cause molecules to jell, and then comes mutation
To create Life in all it's diversity,
Millions of species, shaped by adversity;
Microbes and fish lead to apes, then Humanity?
I must have been suffering from gross insanity!

In the fullness of time, in the open sky,
You'll see a herd of pigs (because now they can fly!).
This will not happen till Man's found the solution,
Then he'll call it the Theory of Evolution …

Holgate Versus Guest.

[Grammar School inter-House rugby. 1958]

'It's heads,' says Pasher, 'Choose your goal!'
So Parkin heels another hole,
Places oval ball just right,
Then kicks it into studied flight.

Hordes of yellow jerseys charge,
And some of them are rather large;
Baker says, 'Why pick on me and not the others?'
He drops the ball and can't recover.

He's on the ground and he's attacked
By friend and foe — a scrum's been stacked!
He mutters, 'Rugby I detest;
I've only come here as a Guest!'

He scrambles out from underneath
The heaving, grunting pile of beef.
'Get in that scrum,' shouts Valentine,
'Or Holgate colours will be thine!'

The ball pops out, and guess who's there
To pick it up? 'It isn't fair,
To put me on the spot like this!'
Says Baker, with a cunning hiss.

With deep dismay the Guest players wince.
'He's gone and given it to Hince!'
Shouts Daley with a face that matches
His big, red shirt with muddy patches.

From Hince to Field, then in a line,
The oval ball is moving fine,
To Clay, Lees, Poskett, Pickin, Pawson —
This Holgate team is really awesome!

Kidd sells Harrison a 'dummy',
Then passes it to Holland's tummy.
He gives the glory all to Morley —
Twigg says to Stonier, 'They do look poorly!'

Baker now has been demoted;
He says, 'I'm safe at full-back.' [quoted]
Then his mind goes into frenzy
As Taylor slips the ball to McKenzie!

McKenzie charges down the wing
With all his fine-tuned muscles pumping;
Baker's shivering with fear:
'It looks like I'm in trouble here!'

Baker runs with all his might,
But it's in the wrong direction. [right?]
McKenzie streaks between the poles
To add to his long list of goals.

Abell, Whalley, Wildman, May,
Gainey, Griffifths, Pickles, say
To Baker when they're, later, showering:
'You've let us all down with your cowering.'

Baker says: 'Well, I don't care,
For none of you would ever dare
To tackle him — that great, big lorry;
I'd rather stay in one piece. Sorry!'

Sefton Youth Club '58

Eyes that glare up at the ceiling;
Grunts and groans and bodies reeling;
Glossy muscles rippling tightly —
Nothing here is taken lightly.

Clanging weights from iron cast;
Repetitions — hope I last;
Straining backs on inclined benches.
What's it for? To please the wenches!

Walls that stream with condensation,
Crumbling from dilapidation,
Pale-green painted, cracked and peeling —
Subsidence there's no concealing.

Training's done, I hear the sound
Of Rock And Roll — the ceilings pound.
Tread the stairs to hear the band,
With a 7-Up bottle in my hand.

Swirling petticoats — who's that chick?
I guess I'd better move in quick!
'Subs' are due, old Skipper's here —
It's time for me to disappear …

Magic Moments '58

'Magic Moments' I remember
From my youth in wintertime;
I think it was in late December
When snow flaked thickly to the ground
As Patricia's birthday party ended,
And from her home we brightly wended.

'Wake Up little Susie', too,
Was current then; perhaps the autumn?
Sue's daddy sang it, just for Sue —
His way of showing her affection.
Miners had an oblique fashion,
When displaying their paternal passion.

And me? I revelled in my new-found senses;
My black crêpe shirt and white sports coat;
But puberty brings consequences,
Which at the time seemed so remote.
The thrill, and knowing that I could
'Pull' pretty girls, felt really good.

It was the start of everything
That gives fulfilment of a kind;
But innocence comes to an ending
That leaves one with a troubled mind.
I sometimes wished I could have stayed
Forever in those halcyon days …

She's Dead?

Memories came flooding back of things *we only* knew:
How summer nights beneath the stars were meant for just
us two.
With constellations in her eyes, and dew drops in her hair,
Our passion knew no ending, and we didn't have a care.

Something told me in my heart I never would forsake her,
And as our spirits intertwined, we didn't need Our Maker.
But she was young and so was I — too young to settle
down,
And love soon loses lustre. She sold her wedding gown.

She still lived within my heart, and often I would grieve,
Although I never did regret it — I just knew I had to leave.
Before she died she told a friend she'd known True Love
once only;
But he'd found better things to do, and she'd been left so
lonely.

When I was told of her last wish, 'Don't take me into
church,'
My heart filled up with tears, I cried: 'There's nowhere I
can search!'
But perhaps she was alone, and perhaps she changed her
mind,
And she asked God for forgiveness as she left this world
behind.

Dancing Dilemmas

She never did learn how to jive,
And never will at fifty-five,
And though she still has charm and grace,
They're better at a slower pace.

The quickstep, foxtrot — perhaps, no,
Though she insists and has a go;
The waltz she is quite suited to —
And there are other things to do.

Country dancing — if it's slow,
Perhaps a samba or a tango.
If she overdoes the Latin style,
She'll finish in a dreadful pile.

As for me, I guess I'll take
Young Rachel — lord, how she could Shake!
She could Mash Potato too,
And make the other girls feel blue.

I never saw *her* ball-room dancing —
All that style and all that prancing!
All *she* knew was how to smooch
[And a little Hoochy-Cooch].

Oh halcyon days why do I only ever find
You in my retrospective mind

Brink of Eternity

Have you ever been there, on the brink
Of the Chasm of Eternity?
It's a place that makes you think,
Amid that calm serenity.
When your spirit hovers over,
And casts its gaze upon
Your mortal body as another's,
So obvious does it become,
That spirits dwell in other realms
Which have not four dimensions.
Eternity quite overwhelms,
As it calls for our attentions.

I had no promise in my heart,
And I knew where I was going;
The time for setting me apart
Had come — to reap what I'd been sowing.
I did not regret a thing I'd done
Or promise I'd do better,
Just this: all opportunities had gone,
And I was still a debtor.
Some say they saw a bright light
At the end of a dark tunnel;
What I felt was lonely fright,
As I fell into the funnel.

All was darkness in this space
Yet despite all this I saw
Two hollow eyes set in a face
That promised: 'There's *no more*.'
No screaming — not a shout,
Nor hope of anything at all;
Then the Devil spat me out
And said, 'Your taste is gall!'
For two decades I thought on this,
The cause of my ejection,
Then Jesus said, 'You're mine — not his,'
As he offered me salvation.

The Promise

She came to haunt me in my dreams,
From forest glens and Highland streams;
Her innocence helped show to me
The man I really ought to be.
A Daughter of the Campbell clan,
She'd often wondered what was God's Plan
For her, and what He wanted her to do
For Him while living here beneath the blue
Skies He'd created.
Although impatient, she had waited.

A nanny — it was just a start,
To find her way and play a part
In domestic life at Bodley Hall,
Until she heard a different call.
I knew not then of how she'd be
A part of my own destiny;
Forever locked within my mind,
Her memory, so sweet, a kind
Of bliss.
I see God's hand at work in this.

Brown hair tousled by the wind,
Determined brow and stubborn chin;
Her nose would wrinkle in disdain
(At times I was a *little* vain);
But eyes that flashed with firm intent
Would soften when her fire was spent,
And something sweet and tender followed,
Moments special, ever hallowed;
Her freckled nose
I loved to kiss, when in repose.

We talked of God, whom I knew not then;
If I could go back there again,
I'd tell her that *my* faith had foundered,
(Which was in Evolution grounded).
If I had tried to keep in touch,
In times of trouble, be her crutch,
Perhaps I could have saved her from
Some of the grief that was to come;
For, with hind-sight,
I know that *she* was right.

But time moves forward with no reverse,
And her calling was — to be a nurse.
I *couldn't* ask for her to stay,
And Glasgow seemed so far away;
So I chose to cherish in my mind,
A memory of a different kind,
That would not fade, was chaste and pure.
I promised her, and I was sure,
We'd meet again,
Though knowing not of how, or when.

Three decades passed and I had found
That her own God to *me* was bound.
I felt a need (I knew she'd prayed)
To tell her that I too was saved.
I travelled North to Craig Duin,
Searched the graveyard for her kin;
Haunted places where we went —
Anything to find the scent
Of her alone.
No one knew where she had gone.

I often do things my own way,
Forgetting that I ought to pray;
A further six years slowly passed
Before God answered me, at last.
A Web that is of Man's devices,
Full of infinite surprises,
This wonderful and splendid tool
Gave me access to her old school.
Its web-page Roll
Enabled me to reach my goal!

I smiled as I read of her 'emigration',
For Inverness is her location:
'Still propping up the NHS',
Same old Rachel — more or less.
I wrote, 'Hi Rachel, do you remember
Nineteen sixty-six, December,
Our farewell kiss upon the doormat?
And my promise to you that
We'd meet again?
Well, here I am — your faithful friend!

Her soul had been through darkest night
Where God seemed absent in her plight
And, though her loving spouse was near,
Everything that she'd held dear
Had turned to ashes in her sight.
Within her grief she'd found a Light,
So different from the one before —
A Universal Faith that helped her more
Than previous belief;
And this new Light gave her relief.

These tidings were so unexpected,
But our friendship, still, was resurrected.
I told her of my darling wife;
My son and daughters, of my life.
Reciprocation was *her* theme;
The months passed by as in a dream.
Then the flame that we'd rekindled
Flared suddenly, and then dwindled
To an ember.
But it still glows — and I *will* remember.

.

Epilogue

I know a secret that I must share,
Look in the Scriptures, it's written there
That Jesus will not lose one sheep;
His promises he vowed to keep.
The Bible says that God planned all,
He even knew of when we'd fall
And lose our faith in Him through doubt —
He promised *He* would sort it out;
For Faith is written in the heart,
The contract's there right from the start.
My consolation:
I know that *nothing* thwarts pre-destination!

Postscript

I often think of this, I find,
That when you were in troubled mind,
Something made me look for you;
And *I* felt desolation, too.

End

The Final Bell

The Final Bell will toll when God decrees,
And His Verdict's based on what he sees.
For he who thinks he'll past the test,
Because he always did his best,
The Ten Commandments, plain and true,
Are waiting there, my friend, for you.

If you can say: '*I did not covet*'
You'll find it difficult to prove it.
If you've never sinned, then you're mistaken.
Jesus never did, but he was taken
To a cross prepared for him,
So he could suffer for *our* Sin.

He paid for mine — I know that's true;
He suffered just as much for you;
But only souls who see the need
For God's own Son to endure and bleed,
And pay that truly awesome price,
Will win the Cross of sacrifice.

My One True Friend,
Kept *all* Commandments to the end!

My Baby's Dead

They say my little baby's dead,
And that is why he lays so still.
I longed to see him in my bed,
But now I know I never will.

I've only seen him on a scan,
His smile was plain to see on there;
Such a darling little man,
Without a worry or a care.

He'll never know of grief and sorrow,
Or what it is to loathe and hate;
He'll never fear about tomorrow
Or ever worry that he's late.

Perhaps he's better off this way,
Without experiencing life;
For, though he'll never seen the light of day,
He'll never know the pain of strife.

But I want to hold him to my breast —
I cannot just forget and sleep;
For though they say it would be best,
I only want to lie and weep.

Lovely Spirits Never Fade

I caress her cheek,
And I find it to be
As smooth,
And as soft
As damask rose-petals
In the early morning.

One day her skin will wrinkle ...

I look into her eyes,
And I see sapphires
Shimmering
In a setting of white,
Polished ivory
Framed with long,
Sweeping lashes,
And the Sisters of Pleides
Twinkle and dance in them
When she smiles at me.

They will grow dull and glazed...

Her smile — oh, her crimson smile
That beckons
Me to kiss
Her honey-laden lips!

*It will become thin
and her lips will lose their fullness of flesh ...*

Her hair is as black
As a raven's wing,
And it tumbles
To her shoulders
Like angry rivers in the night

And,
When she turns her head to speak,
Her curls gently eddy and swirl
About her white neck.

It will turn grey and grow brittle...

When she speaks,
I can feel the blood
Coursing through my veins,
And my heart beats
Along with every syllable;
When she sings,
The angels lay down their harps
To listen,
And they nod to each other
In silent agreement.

Her voice will become dry and shrill...

Her body moves
With the grace
Of a slender willow
That sways
In sweet harmony
With its own moon-cast shadow
In a warm, summer evening breeze.

Her bones will stiffen, and she will lean forward
with the weight of her many, coming years ...

She may grow old
And, one day,
All these things
Will rot
And wither in the grave,
But her *spirit* will live

Forever in my soul —
And *that* will never fade.

How I love her spirit!

The Simple Things in Life

We hurry and scurry — and what is it for?
Material things, we just want more and more
To fill up the void, for they lose their attraction,
Sometimes as soon as we've made the transaction.

Let's forget all the things that our money can do —
I'm happy hanging around with just you.
Let's look at the stars that have been there forever
And think of eternity, now we're together.

Perhaps we can stay till we see the dawn break
And the sun rises over that beautiful lake,
As it has done since time began, all of those years;
No need for sorrow and no need for fears.

Eternity rolls on without you or I —
So what is the point of the things that we buy?
This pleasure we have is both simple and free,
Yet nothing compares with you being with me.

Cuddles

When we get into a muddle
There is nothing like a cuddle,
To ease the pain and gratify the senses;
But proximity arouses
Something different in our spouses,
And there always seem to be such consequences.

Well ... I've gone and got a cat
So I can do away with that —
Cuddles only asks for 'Whiskas' and attention.
He now strokes me with his paws,
I need not speak of menopause —
Nor other things I do not wish to mention!

Bob Taylor has also contributed to Northern Lights,
a collection of poems and stories from emerging authors,
to be published in May 2007

Other books from Magpies Nest Publishing

When Phones Were Immobile
and Lived in Red Boxes
An illustrated book of childhood memories 1939-1953
By Gladys Hobson
ISBN 0-9548885-0-2

Blazing Embers
A tale of mature love.
By Angela Ashley
ISBN 0-9548885-2-9

When Angels Lie
all hell is let loose and demons fly!
By Richard L Gray
ISBN 0-9548885-1-0